Promote Yourself
What's Holding You Back?

Doris Gaines Rapp, Ph.D.

Copyright 2013 Doris Gaines Rapp, Ph.D.

ISBN: 978-0-692-01895-8

Daniel's House Publishing

P.O. Box 623

Huntington, Indiana 46750

This book is dedicated to all those who are afraid to promote themselves, their work and their talents.

Permit Success – Promote Yourself

**To order *Promote Yourself*

go to: www.amazon.com

http://www.bn.com**

TABLE OF CONTENTS

Preface
Confidence Builder and Permission Giver
"Shameless" Self-Promotion
Self-Promotion with Positive Body Language
Times Have Changed
Reasons some People Are Afraid to Self-Promote
Differences Between Men and Women and How that May Affect Their Ability to Self-Promote
What Do You Need or Want to Promote?
That's Not a Talent of Mine!
Barriers – Ways You Sabotage Your Own Success
Possible Why Not(s)
Validation from Others
You Do Not Need Others to Validate You
What is Keeping You from Promotion Yourself?
Convincing Another
Just a Thought
Begin by Beginning
Where(s)
Review
Conclusion – P.S.
References

PREFACE

I won't waste your time by reviewing what you already know. This book will not discuss the *where* of promoting yourself. The cyber-world has bombarded us with the *where* of self-promotion: websites, blogs, Facebook, LinkedIn, Twitter and Goodreads; of course there are college placement services, networking with other professionals you have met in the field, contacts with family and friends, writers' conferences, job fairs, and apprentice or internship placements; and don't forget unique and creative resumes (avoid the pretty pink paper), face-to-face interviews and presentations, head-hunters, cold calls and so much more I can't keep up with it all. Perhaps you investigated them all – "Way to go you!"

This small book addresses just one issue.

It's a pep-talk on self-promotion.

Not, "Where do I promote?" But, "Why am I not?"

Why are you afraid to promote yourself?

What are your stumbling blocks?

For those of you who are reading this book as an eBook, keep a computer window open to your word processing program to take notes and give responses, write on 3X5 cards or use a small notebook.

CONFIDENCE BUILDER AND PERMISSION GIVER

If you have purchased this book or are part of one of my *Promote Yourself* seminars, write in it or take external notes and pass the book on to a friend.

This book has one purpose: to help you gain the confidence to promote yourself, your fresh degree, your new idea, your newly opened office or business, your new book, or your newly created product.

We will not develop a marketing plan or look at a needs assessment for whatever you are promoting—yourself or your product. There are many others who can do that for you and will be glad to help. But, if you cannot or will not promote yourself, marketing will be a slow-go or a no-go.

This book is to enable you to face the reality of business in the twenty-first century. After the product is completed, the degree earned, the marketing plans are all in place, whatever the preparation has been, a new reality is still there.

"Of course you know you will have to promote yourself." It doesn't matter if your product is *you*, an invention, a new business, a novel, a promotion at work, or a program at

church, work or school—the one who will need to convince others of its worth is—YOU!

"SHAMELESS" SELF-PROMOTION

Don't mistake a business decision to promote your work with shameless self-promotion. The term "shameless self-promotion" refers to stealing the spot-light from others to place yourself center stage.

- "You think that's funny, listen to what happened to me last week."
- "I know your street improvement program is a nice little start, but when I worked for Mr. Big, we re-routed all the belt-ways around Dallas."
- "That might work, Mike—oh sorry, Mick. But, you're thinking small. Let's look at the bigger picture."
- "What a nice, plain blue interview outfit. My grandmother had one just like it."
- "Well, you know Stevie Boy, the golf team this company has is serious business. I was on the championship team my junior and senior years in college. Sorry, maybe you can find something else to do."

Think of a time when you had over-promoted yourself – shameless self-promotion. Write a few words that will help you hold that picture in mind.

_____

_____

_____

_____

_____

How do you feel about that event now?

_____

_____

_____

What could you have done or said differently?

_____

_____

_____

This book is not about promoting oneself in a rude or obnoxious way—shamelessly. Self-promotion is vastly different in our context.

It is very difficult for some people to see that difference. From the time they were small, they were taught it's wrong to out-shine others. One must win graciously and keep most accomplishments to themselves, so they don't sound like they're bragging. It is very sad when they have no one with whom to share their achievements and their joy, because others in their family or circle of friends do not have similar accomplishments, or they believe they don't.

That is not self-promotion. That is self-deprecation. Self-promotion is your opportunity to provide someone with something they already need. You are doing them a service.

It is the very thing that marketing experts did for Henry Ford, Sloan-Kettering Hospital, or Dan Brown—author. Unless you are one of those guys, or a large business, **you** are the only one who will be able to let the world know you have something they need or would enjoy.

There is nothing new about what I have written on these few pages. You can read multiple books on self-help, self-improvement, or earn a Ph.D. in Psychology. You can gain all the knowledge you want. If you write a book about your discoveries, you will still have to promote it. If you invent a new mouse trap, it is your responsibility to promote it. If you have a shiny new degree, you are the one who will have to present yourself for employment.

So . . . Promote Yourself.

SELF-PROMOTE WITH POSITIVE BODY LANGUAGE

"When is the bookstore open?" a young seminary student asked. He had hurried onto campus early so he could buy his books and possibly a cup of hot coffee. He didn't have time to re-check the store after classes. He had a wife and three children, served a church twenty miles away, and was a full time seminary student.

"Sorry. The bookstore has no manager yet so it's only open in the evening when someone can leave the office and open it," a secretary apologized.

"If you're still looking for someone, I'll manage it for you." He flashed his usual friendly and confident smile and stood tall.

"Have you had any experience?" she asked.

"I managed the school bookstore when I was a senior in high school. We sold books, paper, candy bars...you know. I placed the orders as supplies ran low."

It was all true. However, he didn't mention the fact that the "bookstore" wasn't much larger than a supply closet. He may have used the theory of successive approximations—

he reported a truth that approached the example the listener assumed he meant. Would he be able to handle the larger bookstore? He had worked since he was fourteen years old. He wasn't afraid to take on a new challenge and work through the learning phase while on the job.

Did he lie? Of course not. Did he over represent himself? Not really. What he said was true and he had ideas for expanding the offerings of the bookstore. It wasn't a large store but he had thought about adding coffee and doughnuts for commuting students. It was a win/win situation. It never occurred to him that he wouldn't be able to do the job, so self-doubt never came through. He presented himself as a success, and they believed he was.

Square your shoulders. Look the employer in the eye and speak with confidence.

The non-verbal language of the fellow below would cause an employer to not trust him with the key to the janitor's closet. His obvious lack of confidence and aura of weakness and failure are visible to everyone he meets.

Remember—show confidence by your posture and bearing. You don't have to know everything. Don't be afraid to ask questions. That is the sign of an inquisitive mind, eager to learn and secure enough in themselves to ask questions.

Look over your stack of pictures that include shots of yourself. Notice your posture. What does it tell you about your feelings the day someone took the picture?

_____

_____

If you pretend that you know what you obviously do not, your lies could catch up with you. Your non-verbal cues, your "tell," will give you away. Does this guy look confident and knowledgeable?

What is your "tell" when you are bluffing?

_____

_____

Prepare carefully. Study the business for which you are interviewing, the products and the history of the company. Know the interviewer's name but use Mr., Mrs., Ms., or Dr. Review what you have to offer the company so they can see how you would fit into their program.

If you've written a book or have an art portfolio, make sure you have reviewed the content. As strange as it may seem, you may have written another book and six articles, or decorated ten buildings with your art since you finished the novel or advertising displays you are presenting on that interview date. It would be quite embarrassing if you couldn't recall the villain's name or the tag line of your art rendering. You might give away your ineptness if you presented the following body language.

What do you have to offer? How would you catch someone's ear if you only had time to deliver one sentence? ONE SENTENCE! What is your single self-promotion statement that defines your work? Work and re-work your statement until it says it all!

_____
_____
_____
_____
_____
_____
_____
_____

TIMES HAVE CHANGED

It seems that this current crop of fresh graduates is more assertive and more willing to present themselves or their program or product to the employer or public. Some get ahead of themselves and look like this. They bombard the interviewer with their brilliance and ability.

Some are so excited by their self-importance their self-cheerleading can become irritating and turn off the very one they are trying to impress.

They need to pace themselves and be energetic and polite. They need to listen at least as much as they talk and have fun with the professional contact.

They are ready, or so it would seem.

REASONS SOME PEOPLE ARE AFRAID TO SELF-PROMOTE

I will identify several individuals and their descriptors and how they might benefit from this presentation due to their reluctance to self-promote.

- There are some people who come from a home of professionals. One might assume that the children and other relatives are similar in personality. While personality characteristics do run in families, it does not mean that the offspring will be like their parents. The children may hide their true personality because they believe they cannot measure up to a parent. Or, they may distort their personality to make themselves more like other family members so they can fit in. Just because Dad or Mom can nail an interview, does not mean the children have the same confidence. In some cases, their parents' assertiveness may cause them to hide in the shadows.

- Sometimes, a person can be the first in their family to go to college, or the first to graduate, or even the first to graduate from high school. Since no one has gone before them, they have no mentors or role models within the family. They will benefit from direction from community friends: a teacher, pastor, neighbor or extended family member, to help them walk through the college application process, advise them on military choices or job seeking.

• Between those two benchmarks is almost everyone else. This book is for all of us.

• Another unique group of people are young women from religious families as compared to men from the same family units.

• Men from homes of faith are to be the head of the family: solid, secure, and assertive. They are to seek God's will for their lives and follow through with the confidence that they are obeying God's calling.

• Women are to be modest, obedient, to place the men and children in their lives first, and to not promote themselves.

• Another group we cannot ignored is the assertive and qualified men, who have gone from one job interview to another and have been unable to successfully find a job within their training and education. They have finally given up all hope of finding their "dream" job. They are not lazy. They simply haven't been able to shift down their gears and expectations to re-connect with the part-time job they had in high school or college summers to provide income while they job hunt. They remain stunned and need a jump-start to re-set their goals.

These good, well-educated workers need to be encouraged into success. Young women must be able to use their education and find an identity of success. Both groups will need to promote themselves, their education and their abilities.

Men and women who are looking for work and/or are ready to begin to self-promote, need to remind themselves that they are people of value.

How would you like others to see you?

_____

_____

_____

What would you like your spouse to know about you?

_____

_____

_____

What would you like your children to know about you?

_____

_____

_____

What would you like for an employer or co-workers to know about you—that is not too revealing?

_____

_____

_____

DIFFERENCES BETWEEN MEN AND WOMEN AND HOW THAT MAY AFFECT THEIR ABILITY TO SELF-PROMOTE

Gail Sheehy has written extensively about the *Passages* people cross during their lives and their identity development. In a pdf document listed at the end of this book, Ms. Sheehy has included a chapter, *Why Can't a Woman Be More like a Man and A Man Less like a Racehorse?* An investment of your time while reading her books may be beneficial to you.

Sheehy believes that men take the independence they feel, or can talk others into believing, and go out into the world and find their identity based on a preconceived time table or step-by-step plan. With each step come honors, awards, appreciation, accolades, and the positive reinforcement that informs and forms his identity. He *is* his job.

Step One: Graduate from college with an appropriate major, well-chosen friends, mentors, and contacts.

At the present time, there are many college graduates who are not able to find the jobs they seek. One can easily see that Step One needs revision. There has been very little in their background or training to help them re-think their lives.

Step Two: Secure a law-clerk position in a prestigious law firm. Or, find an entry-level job in a business of their interest.

If the gradate has not accomplished Step One, Step Two is delayed, along with the beginning of their identity development as it relates to their career.

Step Three: Achieve Junior Partner by age thirty. Or, advance to manager in the business by the same age.

The graduate's ability to succeed in life will depend on their flexibility. Those who cannot adapt to their situation will only stagnate.

Step Four: Make Senior Partner by age forty. Or, rise to CEO or start his own business by then.

If our graduate has been adaptable to his needs, he may be as successful as the Senior Partner or CEO. The measure of his success will be for him to determine on his own.

If a woman marries right out of college, or at least in her twenties, she does not have the same time table or plan as her husband, or other women who have not chosen to marry. She divides her "time" between home, husband, children and work. Where a man must build up his business opportunities, married women and moms must still put their careers second to their family. She must know who she is *before* she can go out and find her independence. Often, she bases her identity on what other people tell her about herself and the longer she is out of the work place, the less her identity is informed and the less confidence she has.

If a woman has chosen to stay home and give the children a good start, she will benefit herself if she has a part-time job, a volunteer position, or has a small creative business. While she creates something to sell, she is getting positive feedback that validates her work and identity.

If you are a man who has had to re-launch his career, or a woman who has not yet begun and has grown apprehensive, this book covers the most important concept.

There are physicians who would like to get out of medicine but can't; lawyers who wish they could find other work; and teachers who do not like teaching. If you are patient with yourself as you re-direct your career, begin again, or carve out a new way of living your productive life, you can become the very best you, not the identical cookie cutter professional you thought you wanted to be. Remember:

- You are accomplished in something or are a willing learner.
- You have something to offer.
- You have every right to promote yourself.
- **You can do it!**

WHAT DO YOU NEED OR WANT TO PROMOTE?

You have just opened an insurance office, a hair salon, an independent law office, day-care center, bicycle shop, restaurant or investment office. You have joined a local church congregation, the Rotary Club and the Better Business Bureau. You want to do more to inform the public about your product or business but are afraid people will think you're coming on too fast and too strong. How do you handle those fears?

Or, the opposite may be true—you don't think you have anything to promote. Perhaps you're happy living in Mom and Dad's basement for a few more years. Calculate your lost earnings while playing games to see if that's a good idea.

If it works—keep it up. If it doesn't—stop it.

Maybe you have a job, so what is the need to convince others about something? It could be that you have a prestigious degree already. There are many reasons for self-promotion. Perhaps you want to promote:

• A Discovery. Remember, you may find a cure for cancer, but if you don't tell anyone or find backers (to promote your discovery) it will benefit no one.

• Yourself. You own one of those independent offices or businesses listed above and have no corporate structure behind you to promote your opening. Perhaps, you are one of sixteen job applicants and they tailored the position just for you. You will have to be successful in telling the employer what you have to offer the company.

• A Book. You have written your first novel and you're looking for a publisher. You know that the publishing business is very tight now and, before you can get near an editor, you have to first secure a literary agent. So you have to promote yourself to an agent, before you can promote yourself to an editor, before you can promote your book to the world.

Write down a few things that you want or need to promote.

_____

_____

_____

THAT'S NOT A TALENT OF MINE!

Maybe you don't like to be in the center of the spotlight, even for an interview hour. You may feel out of your element. You may believe you just cannot do something so foreign to your personality.

I agree. It may feel uncomfortable. Your personality may not attend to detail or even use logic in making decisions. You may not be business-like at all and yet you realize self-promotion is part of doing business.

Many years ago, I had the privilege of interviewing Catherine Marshall in her wonderful farmhouse in the beautiful Shenandoah Valley of Virginia. After our interview, I had asked her if she ever got involved in her husband's publishing business. She said, "Oh, my no. Publishing and writing are two entirely different talents."

That is exactly what all of us must do in today's scene, whether it is promoting a new business, book, scientific discovery, or a new type of air purifier for coal mines. We have to step out of our profession or comfort zone and use talents we never had—self-promotion. (Note: I got the interview with Catherine Marshall by simply calling her on the telephone.) We must deliberately do what we do not naturally do.

There are many programs that help us determine our strengths and secondary talents (not weaknesses—that's negative self-talk). While we lead with our strengths, we are more well-rounded and able to talk to people of different types, or succeed at different tasks, when we develop our secondary talents too.

The Myers-Briggs Personality Type Indicator is such a test. The test results in one of sixteen, four-letter personality types. It can help identify careers for which your talents may be an asset, and interview styles. The "Personality Pages" link below can identify some of that information. For our purposes here, your "type" helps you understand your strengths as well as those secondary skills that can be developed and called on when you need to complete a task that is outside your normal comfort zone.

You can take the full test at a University Career Center and many counseling offices. A quick, four question mini-test is on the "Personality Pathways" link listed in the References section at the end of the book.

The "Personality Pages" link below gives a list of possible careers that may fit your personality type. It is fun to look at and you can expand your thinking to include similar jobs to the ones listed.

Another reviewed site, gave the four-letter personality type but the list of possible job interests was very limiting. They asked one to choose which of a pair of activities they preferred, when neither was a high priority. You end up with career possibilities that are below the expectations of most college graduates. I suggest the mini-test to give you a quick look at your personality type and then apply that four-letter code to the career preference based on personality type included on the "Personality Pages" link.

When you learn to take in information by your senses—what you see, hear etc.—not just your intuition, and make value judgments about that information based on logic and not just feelings, you will be able to deliberately apply secondary skills and accomplish far more than you thought you could. Of course, the reverse of those traits is also true.

Other reasons you may need to promote are:

• A New Product: Perhaps you have spent years planning, perfecting and building a final model of your invention. It's done! Now, there it sits in your garage or lab because promotion is not one of your talents. If you don't have the funds to hire a marketing firm and/or sales team to promote your new revolutionary product, no one will know about it or benefit from your gift.

• A New Program: There is a wonderful advancement possibility at work if you can develop a new sales program to provide affordable insurance to newly graduated college students using social networking as a means of getting the connections started, thus saving on sales personnel. Or, you have to convince the church board about an opportunity to meet the needs of young families in your community, by forming a free after-school program, utilizing the facilities of the church building.

• A Point of View or Opinion at Home: You are married to a loving spouse who has the habit of expecting you to justify why you want something.

> Spouse says, "I'd like to go to the mountains for our vacation this summer."
>
> You say, "I'd like to go to the beach."
>
> Spouse says, "The beach? Why? Give me three very good, mind-changing reasons why we should go the beach." He provided no reasons for his choice.

• New Parenting Rules: There has been entirely too much time spent in the house on computer games and too little time out in the fresh air and sunshine. Household chores need to be re-assigned and homework hours have slipped. You will present your ideas to your children at the family meeting tonight. The same principles of promotion apply here.

There are as many reasons why we promote something as there are individuals who must promote. Make peace with that fact. Promote Yourself.

BARRIERS—WAYS YOU SABOTAGE YOUR OWN SUCCESS

It is certainly self-defeating to think that one would sabotage their own efforts to succeed. That's not possible! Why would anyone harm their own efforts to achieve the very thing they claim they want?

Perhaps they are deceiving themselves. Maybe they do not really want what they think they do. How might they sabotage their efforts?

1. Many people simple do not complete their project. They may not finish their book, their plans for the new program, or their resume.

> a. While engaged in psychotherapy at a university counseling center, I had a very bright student who decided she didn't want to graduate. I told her she didn't have to. I suggested she might go ahead and register to march with her class, so if she changed her mind, she would be prepared. She could take some creative classes the following year and have some fun. Given the option of not graduating was all she needed to make the

decision to wear the gown and mortar board on that special spring day.
2. You might deliberately do a poor job on your interview, presentation, or brochure so you have a built-in excuse for the failure you fully expect will happen.
   a. I didn't really have the time to get it all done the way I wanted to.
   b. The endnotes? They had to be a specific format? Sorry.
   c. The drawings should have been in days ago—I know. I tried.
3. One might have a fear of success. If they make that great movie, or write the break-out novel, they'll have to follow it with an even better sequel. Their fear—"What will people expect of me now?"
   a. "Book two? I know I have another thriller in me, but I just can't think of it now."
   b. Fear of Success in selling: "Sure, I'll sell the first condo in one week and the rest of the units in two months. Oh, no, I forgot. I will be out of town this Fall just when you want to launch the campaign. I didn't realize you needed that long of a time commitment when we first talked."
4. There could be a fear of failure. So they don't try. They may get to use the old, trite phrase, "I knew I wouldn't make it all along."
   a. "You just have to help me, Willard. I may be in over my head."

POSSIBLE WHY NOT(s)

Why do we have these fears? We secretly speak truths or lies about ourselves based upon perceptions we have gained from how others have treated us and spoken to us. We believe what they have said about our successes and failures, and form false-truths about whether what we are doing has meaning.

Those internal messages dictate our actions and emotions. If you believe you can't succeed, you will not attempt to promote a "looser." You will not try.

If you think your beliefs teach you to be modest and quiet, you'll make sure you do not "shine." You will not "push" yourself into leadership and you won't speak first, so . . . you will not promote yourself.

Negative self-talk is caustic to our confidence. Some messages you may have heard are:

- Who do you think you are?
- You're no better than anyone else.
- Polite people don't self-promote.

- An expert needs to recommend or validate your work.
- Dad said you'd never make it.
- Mom was gone all of the time. It's her fault.
- Men are too aggressive.
- If you promote yourself, you are aggressive too.

Many people don't even know the meaning of aggression. Let's look at the three positions of interacting in the world.

1. *Non-assertion* is when you need something but you let others walk all over you when you try to gain it.

2. *Assertion* is when you need something and go about meeting your goals without walking on others.

3. *Aggression* happens when you need something and walk on others and hurt them in order to get what you want.

Self-promotion is not aggression. It is not the act of promoting your own interests above others' needs. You don't attack another sporting goods store to lift up your own.

Self-promotion is doing the marketing of your product yourself because our economy is not robust enough for someone else to take a chance on a new product, expand a business to include a fresh face unless you convince the company to do so, or invest in the publication of a new author in a time when small and intermediate publishing houses are closing or selling out to large conglomerates. There are very few entry positions in many fields, leaving those seeking their own way to create their own opportunities.

Enter: the indie-screen writer, the indie-film maker, the indie-author, or the indie-CEO/POC (President of their Own Company) – the self-employed.

List five self-messages you rehearse that keep you from promoting yourself, your ideas and/or your creations.

1. _____
2. _____
3. _____
4. _____
5. _____

Which one scares you the most and why?

_____

_____

VALIDATION FROM OTHERS

Some will not promote themselves without first getting validation from others. If my friends, family, spouse, or other professionals say that my ideas are worthy of hearing, then I can proceed.

In fact, without validation, the individual may then "in-validate" their work, words, or creativity by apologizing for their hard work or ideas that created it.

"Well, it's not that good," which tells the complimenter that their judgment is poor or laughable.

"I *could* have done better." Then, why didn't you? What kept you from it?

"I *should* have done better." What *should* you have done?

"I felt rushed." "I didn't have the money to really do well." These are compliment-seeking statements—digging.

Or worse, a take-back compliment. "Well, now that I think about it, I agree. You should have taken more time, or waited to get more money."

Accept a compliment gracefully. The only response to a compliment is, "Thank you."

"Someone said today, 'If being linked is so great, why aren't we all doing better?'"

1. If I don't feel linked, perhaps I am thinking only of myself.
2. One linking social media site is LinkedIn. If you're like me, you really didn't know how LinkedIn works. I bought, *LinkedIn for Dummies*.

I will see if I understand the process by promoting *Promote Yourself* on LinkedIn and other social media sites. If the process is to pass along needed information about self-promotion to those who may benefit from reading this book, then social media should be the super-highway on which it rides.

YOU DO NOT NEED OTHERS TO VALIDATE YOU

Every Monday, I write a devotional and post it on www.prayertherapyrapp.blogspot.com. I don't have a huge readership but I have readers in many countries around the world.

The post on July 29, 2013 discussed the concept of validation. I have included part of it here. There may be a new blossom in the desert of our ability to self-promote within these few paragraphs.

KNOW WHOSE YOU ARE

"Count yourself blessed every time someone cuts you down or throws you out, every time someone smears or blackens your name to discredit me. What it means is that the truth is too close for comfort and that . . . person is uncomfortable. You can be glad when that happens—skip like a lamb, if you like!—for even though they don't like it, I do . . . and all heaven applauds. And know that you are in good company; my preachers and witnesses have always been treated like this." Luke 6: 22-23 (The Message)

Some might say, "Will you make these points in the meeting [for me]? You are so much better at persuasion than I am."

Some people don't trust their own ideas or speak up for themselves. They are afraid, because someone else has not validated them first. Friends, if God has given you a truth, you need no other validation, for the Lord has trusted you to carry the message—the program idea, the creative work, the invention or the manuscript—to the world around you. You need no other permission or support.

"But, what if I sell only five widgets?" If quantity is how you measure your worth, then five sales could represent a business failure. If obedience to God is your goal, then connecting five people with your invention could be the very mission He has called you to. If you know whose you are, the world's concept of success has no validity in your life.

[A story about Billy Graham that followed gave an inspiring example of how one life that was touched, may be the entire reason for your efforts. I closed with prayer, using the Prayer Therapy model.]

Be obedient. A small window may open, letting in the truth that your words or ideas were important to someone.

> [Update: On 7/28/16, I posted "Be a Uniter not a Divider" on www.prayertherapyrapp. blogspot.com. The statistics of viewership for that post alone were: Russia 21 viewers; France 6; China 5; Japan 4; Germany 2; Romania 2; Latvia 1; and the United States 25,897. What fun was that!!]

WHAT IS KEEPING YOU FROM PROMOTING YOURSELF?

What is step one? It doesn't have to be a big step. Any movement in the right direction is positive.

What first step do you need to take? Tell the truth. Be honest in all transactions and contacts. The most important is: Be honest with yourself.

Sometimes we are **overwhelmed**. We can't see the trees for the forest, the detail from the big picture, or the mess.

If you are overwhelmed and just need to know where the Yellow Brick Road begins, start by setting up goals. You don't begin a new job by identifying your retirement date. You being at the beginning and set some goals.

Short Term Goals

What is something you can do right now, to take the first step?

1. Look up a phone number

2. Find an address

3. Type up your resume

List some small steps you can take to get your self-promotion started:

1._____
2._____
3._____
4._____
5._____

Intermediate Goals

1. Make that phone call
2. Write the letter or email
3. Type up your resume and mail/email some out

List some intermediate steps that might follow.

1._____
2._____
3._____
4._____
5._____

Long-Term Goals

1. With calm energy and confidence, interview for a job. Be honest, polite, humble, and enjoy your time. Believe in yourself completely using an assertive approach.

2. Send a follow-up letter or email, thanking the interviewer for their time. Be sure to mention something about the company that was of particular interest to you.

Examples:

- "I thought your tag-line for your products was fantastic. 'Arm yourself with acme skin cream.' I have used the cream and it really works."

- "You have created an energetic work environment where ideas are shared and welcomed. I would enjoy being part of your team."

Jot down any long-term goals that come to mind.

1._____
2._____
3._____
4._____
5._____

CONVINCING ANOTHER

Convincing another to include you, buy your product, or listen to your opinions has a three stage process. Remember as you read these, they absolutely must be genuine. *If you fake it, you'll break it.*

1. Walk beside them
2. Find common ground
3. Introduce yourself, your products and/or your ideas

Walk beside them

At a recent book signing at a Barnes and Noble Bookstore, they placed the table with my books, pens and eager energy to sell and sign the books beside the NOOK® counter. As people stopped to talk to the clerk I would listen because I was in the market for a newer eReader too. As the customers progressed on down the aisle:

• I engaged them in talk about the NOOK®. (Walked beside them.)

Find Common Ground

• I told them about my small, light-weight Nook® and my reasons for purchasing what I had previously bought. I talked about the new eReader I was thinking of buying, one with color and a larger screen. (Common Ground)

Introduce Yourself and/or Product

• Then, I told them about my book and that it is available in eBook form as well as the paper-backs I had on the table. (I introduced my ideas and product.)

I was pleased with the signing and the opportunity to meet the wonderful readers. My goal was not to sell a case of books. My goal was to promote my book and my name as an author, and perhaps by book three, they may say, "Hey, I've heard of her. I think I met her at Barnes and Noble." A book signing isn't about selling books. It's about meeting readers.

JUST A THOUGHT

Many men grew up in homes with no dad present. There was no one to model masculine behavior and no one to sharpen their antlers on.

They can't find jobs they were educated and trained to do, so their identity lacks sharp definition as in previous eras.

Some find identity in gangs; some in being the high scorer in an eGame, conquering the mountain online, or butting their head against no-one in a game.

They may also begin to find their identity in what others tell them about themselves—like women have done over the years.

Women get their identity from what others tell them and, these days, parents leave that training to advertisements, videos, music, the schools and their children's friends.

People of faith may have inadvertently reverted to nineteen-fifties training on role expectations.

• Dad is the head of the house until the daughter is married.

- Divorce in families of faith who attend church regularly is 38% so Dad may not even be around until the daughters marry.
- Children are seen and not heard.
- Girls are modest and creative but do not self-promote.

Not even the families who believe in this model follow it. Dad doesn't actually make the decisions because he holds down two jobs or works long hours so Mom can stay home and parent the children. She may even home-school them. So, they follow the "Go ask your mother" pattern.

We live in a new millennium in which women work, are creative, and sell their creations. They have to self-promote.

A setback can create doubts but it doesn't have to. A scientist experiments with everything until something works. Each attempt is not a failure. It is a success because they have ruled out one more thing that does not work.

I don't pretend that these few pages will solve your dilemma of being stuck. They offer a shift in paradigm—a new avenue of thought—a pep-talk.

If you are promoting a new product, it doesn't have to be a cure for cancer to make it worthwhile. It is what it is.

The book you have written does not have to be *Pride and Prejudice* or *The De Vinci Code*. It stands on its own merits. It is what it is.

What part does faith play? If God gave you a book, he would want it circulated.

If God inspired you to invent a new mouse trap, he would expect you to promote it.

If God gave you a voice like an angel, he would expect you to share it. Sometimes sharing means self-promoting your websites, records, books, and concerts.

The difference between you and those who are successful is, they believed in themselves enough to self-promote.

It is said, when Rick Warren wrote his book, *Purpose Driven Life*, he self-published it, then bought the first ten-thousand copies and donated them. His philanthropic endeavor created the circumstances that allowed his book to open on a Best Seller list. He believed in his book enough to invest in it and self-promote it. Later, published by Zondervan, it sold millions of copies.

Colonel Harland Sanders believed in his chicken breading recipe enough to promote it and market it, but also, enough to invest in franchises at which to sell the newly branded Kentucky Fried Chicken.

BEGIN TO PROMOTE BY BEGINNING

Call that person you need to reach. They may say, "What in the world are you talking about?"

Use humor to inform them. "Thank you for asking. I am calling to find out if I can set up an appointment to talk to you about my new what's-it." Their rudeness is not about you, it's about them.

It is their job description to talk to your job description. They do it well or they do it poorly.

The concept of a conversation from one job description to another job description is very liberating. If you could review the job description of every profession, I doubt that you would find one that includes - "Be rude" or "Insult the interviewee." Unless, you are looking at the job description for Don Rickles.

Public to New Office or Business in Town

When one opens a new office in town—as under the heading, "What Do You Need or Want to Promote?"—the independent business owner wants to influence (promote) themselves to the public. In that case, it is the public's job description to talk to the indie owner.

The Public's job description is to seek out gifted, competent and amicable businesses from which to secure their goods and services. They are to do business in an honest and even-tempered manner. Friendliness is nice but not required.

The job description of the business owner is the happy task of providing what people need. If the product or service purchased is misrepresented or defective, it is the responsibility of the business owner to make restitution in an honest and even-tempered manner. It is one job description talking to another job description.

In a smaller town, there are friendships and even familial relationships that make the business even more pleasant— if both sides are honest and even-tempered. Self-promotion in these cases is somewhat easier, in that these are goods and services sought by the public. The promotion is to inform the public of their availability.

Editor to Author

Their job description (editor) talks to your job description (author).

When I was a junior in high school I entered a speech contest in which the student could compete with a canned speech written by another and scored on the speech delivery alone. If one were to write their own speech and deliver it, the scoring was on content and quality of the speech as well as the presentation and delivery.

There was a new English teacher/Drama Coach in the building that year who was the advisor for that contest team. I had written my speech and felt quite proud of it. I carried the three-page, single-spaced manuscript to the new teacher in the corner classroom on the second floor north hall.

"Put it here," she said as tapped on the corner of the large wooden desk. "I'll look at it over the weekend. You stop back in after school on Monday and we'll go over it."

Wow, it was that easy. I had completed the masterpiece of creative prose and I couldn't wait for her to tell me how brilliant it was.

The last bell rang at the end of the school day on that following Monday. I was willing to miss the school bus and walk home in order to keep my appointment with the drama coach. I walked quietly into her classroom and approached the desk.

"I'm glad you're here, Doris. I have your paper, so let's talk about it." She took my precious three sheets of paper from the stack and laid them out between the two of us.

That was my first glimpse at my wonderful, bruised and bleeding speech. She smiled encouragingly and pointed to each line crossed out with a red pencil. In the middle of the lower half of the second page was one sentence that remained untouched by the attacker's sword.

"There," she pointed as she got excited about her find. "Now that is a great sentence! Begin there!"

At first I was in shock. What had happened? I had to write a whole new speech.

Of course she was right. I won first place with my new speech in the contest that year and earned a mental-trophy in my ability to respond positively to editing. Not intimidated, it was simply their job description talking to my job description—editor to author. It was never about discouragement or destroying the hopes of a young writer. It was all about making the writing better.

Engineer to Inventor

"Say, George, I've found a solution to the problem the women on my line are having as they try to pound out the peened over tabs on the switch housings," the young group leader said as he flagged down his foreman.

"What ya got?"

"Here, I made a drawing last evening," the on-the-job inventor said as he handed the paper to the boss.

"Looks good," the foreman agreed as he studied the diagram. "Let's get the engineers down here."

Before the end of the shift, two men from the engineering department came by the line. "We've looked at your drawing—of course it's not drawn to scale. We don't think it will work. We worked up a model to show you."

They presented the example from the drawing and placed it on the work table. "See, if you put a component on it, you can't get a hammer in there to straighten the tabs. Nice try, but you'd better leave the inventions to our department."

The group leader took no offence. He had known one of the men in the white shirt and striped tie since the third grade when they competed against each other on the gym floor.

With his usual humor, always remembering to laugh *with* someone not *at* them, he chuckled, "Well, now Clarence, I did leave it to you fellows. I know how busy you guys are. After observing the pattern of the workers, I have come up with a solution. Do you want one of these fourteen women to tell you how much they need for this thing to work? Or better yet, ladies," he turned to the women in his department who still sat working on the line and eager to get out and go home, "tell these talented engineers about your need for a better way to do this job."

With one voice, they chided the "superior intellects" of the tied-ones. "Bill knows what we need. You guys just make it," they jabbed.

It is in the job description of the engineer to listen to the needs and ideas of the people who make the company's products. If they are arrogant and/or rude, those spoken to do not need to feel offended. Their negative attitude does not define their job—therefore; their rudeness is not about the group leader or other factory workers. The negative attitude is about them and their own feelings of inadequacy and fear of failure. Walk beside them, find common ground, and present your ideas.

Professor to Student

Those who study to become psychologists must first earn their undergraduate degree, complete their master's program and complete a prescribed number of classes in their doctorate over the next two to three years before engaging in a twelve-month internship year.

During the first semester of my Internship, one of my clinical supervisors was always late for our supervision hour. I said nothing but made sure I was prompt. I was late a few times the second semester. Again, no comment. When I asked him about a reference I had given him he stated, "You've been late. Your reference is not a high priority for me."

His Job Description: supervision and act as mentor, complete references and recommendations in a timely manner, and model professional behavior.

My Job Description: accept suggestions for improvement with an open mind, come prepared as required, and display professional behavior.

When my supervisor responded to my request for information about a reference, I said calmly, quietly and with professional demeanor, "I didn't know that promptness was important to you since you were late every session during the first semester. And, I understood that getting out references and recommendations on time was part of your job description." He said nothing.

Later I discussed the situation with my training director and requested a different supervisor for the remainder of the year. The professor's behavior and statements shocked him. He immediately assigned me to a different supervisor.

Yes, I could have held my tongue and "suffered through" the rest of the school year. However, my training included learning to take on professional interactions with others. Polite but sure assertiveness is one of them.

Interviewer to Job Applicant

Remember, during an interview, you are interviewing the business at the same time they are interviewing you. An interview is an opportunity for sharing information and for the interviewee to find out if they want to accept the job and work there.

It is not aggressive to ask questions. In fact, intelligent, well researched and thought out questions demonstrate a beginning knowledge of the company where you are interviewing.

Be careful about making suggestions for company improvement at the interview. Rather than being helpful, you may be demonstrating arrogance not appreciated. Innovative ideas are great. But, not the shameless self-promotion we talked about before. I know actors can get by with rude swagger in the movies, but your interview is in real life. If boasting and half-truths are what the company values, you may want to re-think the company as a possible place of employment.

While you want to make sure you are honest, do not reveal too much. It is not part of your job description as the interviewee to be vulnerable or uncomfortable. Do not get angry, even if provoked. Don't take the bait. Know who you are and calmly go about being professional.

Bookstore Manager to Author

I have been having fun writing novels during the last few years. A list of them is at the end of this book. With small and/or indie publishers, and a growing number of larger houses, the author will promote their own books.

Once again, I have talked to some authors who write wonderful books but are very reluctant to promote their work.

I tell writers, "Just pick up the phone and call a bookstore to set up a book signing. All they can say is, 'Lady, are you crazy?'"

"That's exactly what they'll say," some have moaned as they admit their fear of self-promotion.

A book signing does not mean you will sell a lot of books. It would be nice if it did. If you are on the New York Times Bestseller list, you already have a following and the fans will attend a book signing as an opportunity to meet the author they have been reading.

If you are a new author, the people in the store do not know you. However, you will have sent out an announcement of your signing to your friends and family, social network and Twitter account. You may have sent a press release to newspapers in the area and local radio stations.

The store will send out their press release, put a "blurb" about your book and that you will be in their store in their "events" sheet, and put up a poster of your book a week or two before the event.

A book signing is a win/win situation.

1. The store gets to advertise something new and eye-catching and get their brand out before the public again.

2. You get publicity! It is all about getting your name out their—your brand. It is not about how many books you sell. It is a wonderful opportunity for you to meet the public and let them know you are in their reading world.

WHERE(s)

While the "where" of self-promotion is not our aim, not knowing about various social media sites may prohibit your ability to begin. I will add a little about accessing a few sites, to make sure lack of awareness is not a stumbling block to beginning.

Website

You don't need a high priced website builder to have a presence on the internet. You can develop your own website. There are several web-building sites in our rapidly expanding world of eCommerce. My only experience is with the construction program I used when I created my site— www.dorisgainesrapp.com. I can update it at any time, add photos and events. With the addition of Pay-pal, I can receive money for online purchases. The site uses templates around which to build your information. Templates are pre-designed background pictures in bright colors or exotic dark tones, with various sections already measured and divided on your screen. The monthly fee is very small—reasonable even in my world. Go to my blog, www.promoteyourself-permitsuccess.blogspot.com, and click on the green words: "**1and1 Website Building.**" It's under, "Build Your Own Website—Follow 1and1 below" in the right column. You will go directly to their website.

Your computer will not explode if you log onto the site and look around. You can add the elements you need, upload pictures, create links, all of it, as you simply select a gadget button. A wonderful twelve-year-old in your life would be able to help you if needed. Lack of big-bucks for a website should not be a stumbling block. You can do it.

Twitter

You can set up a Twitter account in minutes at www.twitter.com. I have no time to tweet every time I see a bird flit through the backyard, but you can make some contacts using the medium. Trust me, if you want a twitter account, you can set one up while the paint dries on the wall or the cookies bake in the oven.

LinkedIn

I will have to admit, I had to purchase *LinkedIn for Dummies* to see what all the whoopla was about. It is a social connection site for professionals and people in business.

There are First-degree connections—people you know; Second-degree network members—people who know at least one of your first-degree connections (friends of friends); and Third-degree network members—friends of your friends' friends.) The chain of connections and network members is vast and long and begins with a friend of yours. Remember the game Six Degrees of Separation? That's LinkedIn. Whether each linking individual actually pays any attention to your current post, I don't know. I am willing to test out the site.

Facebook

There is Facebook for family and friends, and there are Facebook pages for your business. Make sure whatever you post on Facebook is something you will want Grandma to read, she has a Facebook page too you know. Also, any employer you may seek employment from now or in the future can access your posts at any time. If you have no time for Facebook, you can post occasionally and direct people to your website where you have more information.

Goodreads

Authors who are launching their first or fifteenth book may get some exposure on Goodreads. It is a wonderful site to find out what people are reading and what they recommend. An author can offer one or more copies of their new book in the Goodread's "Giveaway" program. The author uploads their information about their book and a "thumbnail" (a jpeg [digital] image of their book's cover). Goodreads gives a daily count-down of the number of days remaining until the date of the give-away—usually a month.

You can post with excitement on Facebook the number of days left to enter. At the end of the pre-determined Giveaway time, Goodreads selects the winner(s) and notifies the author of each winner's name and address so the author can mail out the book(s) to the winner(s). It's easy and exciting to watch the list of readers who enter to win your book grow.

Blogs

Blogs are fun. They are your opportunity to share your opinions on a topic or create a running dialogue on a particular issue. You can post to your blog as often as you want to. People can read your comments from all over the world. I am familiar with Blogspot.com. They charge nothing. I have started a blog as an interactive opportunity for people who want to promote themselves. Those who log on don't often comment, but statistics indicate readership: http://www.promoteyourself-permitsuccess.blogspot.com.

Every Monday, I post a devotional and prayer therapy prayer on http://www.prayertherapyrapp.blogspot.com. These blogs are free and they also use templates. It's not hard—in fact it's creative.

> [Update: Recently, I have serialized one of my novels on www.dorisgainesrapp.blogspot.com. The statistics today indicate 3881 readers have viewed it in the last month with similar numbers per month in the last seven months. While my readers don't rival

those of NY Times best-selling authors, I am very pleased.]

Pinterest

Pinterest is also a free site where you can pin all kinds of interests and share them with others. Each interest topic has its own board (like a bulletin board). My daughter has many boards—recipes and teaching tips are just two.

I have a few. The first one I created was to share pictures of our small country church after a tornado took the roof off and set it down in the farmer's soybean field across the street. People needed a place to see the damage and the restoration.

If you have a computer, you can create any of these. They should not be the reason for not promoting yourself. However, some people do use them as an excuse.

Often, your children and grandchildren are on the computer a lot anyway. Let them show you how to create the sites you need or give them a few dollars to be your webmaster (the one who creates and updates it). They will have fun and can boast a little about having a job as a webmaster.

Find another excuse for not promotion your work, not lack of computer skills. User-friendly is a welcomed word to untrained people like me. The site and programs have to be. If they aren't easy to use, people will find other internet offerings that are user-friendly. Competition helps us all.

REVIEW

We did not talk much about how to self-promote or why to self-promote. We talked about—why not? What are you afraid of?

You are a good and worthwhile person. You are not perfect—none is perfect or we would be God. Trust me, we are not God.

Reasons to Fear Promotion – See if you can spot the emotional theme.

1. Fear of revealing your fear

2. Fear of being laughed at

3. Fear of being ridiculed

4. Fear of failure

5. Fear of success

6. Fear of being judged

7. Fear of being rejected

8. Fear others will discover we really are not good at what we do

9. Fear we will "one-up" our family or friends

10. Fear we will out-grow our loved ones

Some Realities

1. Your family may be the last ones to buy your invention, call your law office if they have a problem, read your book, wear your designs, or buy your insurance.

2. Your friends may not even talk about your achievements. Support of your professional life usually comes from colleagues. Friends are to help you stay grounded.

- You are more than your job or talent anyway.
- Friends help us remember who we are beyond the degree or plaque on the wall.
- If our past is best forgotten, then we have not made peace with our past.
- Your true "fan club" may be people you don't even know.

3. You do no need friends and family to validate your experience. You can know what you know.

Truths

1. Spend more time lifting up other people than in seeking praise.

2. Self-promotion is the other part of your job. It is expected and accepted.

3. What you do not naturally do, you must deliberately do.

- If the business side of your creativity, or the creative side of your business, is not in your nature to do or enjoy, deliberately do it. Deliberately do what you do not naturally do.

- Develop the opposite side of your abilities, the secondary talents. These are the ones we develop in order to talk to people of opposite types or deliberately do the task that is not our first preference or strength. These are the ones that round out our personality and help us to understand others.

4. You do not have to give up your fear. Fear will help you think before you talk and research before you act. Embrace the fear and let its energy fortify you.

Convincing Another

Remember the approach to successfully convince another. It is not magic. You won't mesmerize someone into buying something they don't want. It is however, an honest, amiable approach. There are three steps.

1. Walk beside them

2. Find common ground

3. Present your ideas

A personal example of this process happened one day beside the pool at our condo in Florida. I had heard that the manager of our Phase V cluster of units had kept the Association fees much lower than the other phases. I had not met him until pointed out in the pool area one day as that "grumpy guy over there."

One morning we had taken our little girls to the pool when the grump came over and pointed at the pool rules posted on the wall.

"Have you seen those rules?" he nearly yelled in an angry outburst.

Walk Beside Him: "Yes, thank you. I've read them to the girls often." Stay calm, quiet, friendly, smiling.

Common Ground: I said, "They tell me you're the one we have to thank for keeping our Association fee so low."

"Yes, I am," he stammered.

Present Your Idea: I added, "I want to thank you for your work on our behalf. I sure wouldn't want your job." (My "idea" is to short-circuit and redirect his rant.)

"Thank you," he responded quietly. And, that was the last time he said more than "Good morning," during our remaining visit.

CONCLUSION – P.S.

Give yourself permission to succeed. Permit Success (P.S.)

Self-Promotion is just another step in the process of inventing, training, presenting, interviewing, selling, writing, and anything else you have put work into. Your achievement doesn't have to be the cure for cancer. It may be a new type of diaper rash cream. It has value and others can use it. It may be a new franchise of an existing brand. While the arches might sell the hamburgers, a new insurance office in town, a new boutique, or the manufacture of a new chair design will require promotion.

If you are the manager of a new Burger King, the corporate office will promote the opening. If you open a new independent restaurant, you will have to promote it. No, re-word that. You will get to have the wonderful excitement of promoting it. What a fun-filled adventure!

Permit success—Promote Yourself

Join the conversation; ask questions, post comments at my Facebook page: Doris Gaines Rapp – Author Page.

REFERENCES:

Elad, Joel MBA (2011). *LinkedIn for Dummies*. Wiley Publishing, Inc. Hoboken, NJ

Sheehy, Gail (1976). *Passages*. Bantam Books, N.Y.

Links:
http://www.gailsheehy.com/Game/chapters/WhyCant.pdf (Why Can't Men Be More Like Women and Less Like a Racehorse?) Accessed 8/5/2013

http://www.personalitypathways.com/type-inventory.html (Very quick 4 question test) Accessed 8/6/2013

www.PersonalityPage.com/careers (Common Careers for Personality Type) Accessed 8/6/2013

www.promoteyourself-permitsuccess.blogspot.com

OTHER BOOKS BY DORIS GAINES RAPP

Rapp, Doris Gaines (2000). *The Prayer Therapy of Jesus*. www.amazon.com (a book on Prayer Therapy).

www.prayertherapyrapp.blogspot.com—a weekly devotion based on Prayer Therapy—posted every Monday

Rapp, Doris Gaines (2013). *Escape from the Belfry*. Archway Publishing. Bloomington, Indiana. Available at: www.archwaypublishing.com and www.amazon.com. (the first in the Adam Shoemaker series)

Rapp, Doris Gaines (2012). *Length of Days—The Age of Silence*. Daniel's House Publishing, Huntington, Indiana. www.amazon.com (the **first** in the Length of Days Trilogy)

Rapp, Doris Gaines (2013-14). *Length of Days—Beyond the Valley*. www.amazon.com. (The second in the Length of Days Trilogy)

Rapp, Doris Gaines (2015) *Length of Days—Search for Freedom*. www.amazon.com. (the third in the Length of Days Trilogy)

Rapp, Doris Gaines (1994). *Lincoln's Christmas Mouse*. Daniel's House Publishing Huntington, Indiana. www.amazon.com

Rapp, Doris Gaines (2015) *News at Eleven - A Novel*. www.amazon.com

Rapp, Doris Gaines (2016-2017) *Escape from the Shadows*. Sequel to *Escape from the Belfry*. Fall 2016 or winter 2017.

EVENTS:

There are book signings at various Barnes and Noble Booksellers in several states from time to time. Go to www.dorisgainesrapp.com for locations, dates and times.

For *Promote Yourself* Seminars: contact Dr. Doris Gaines Rapp at dorisgainesrapp@gmail.com. For information, go to www.dorisgainesrapp.com

www.ingramcontent.com/pod-product-compliance
Lightning Source LLC
Chambersburg PA
CBHW051957290426
44110CB00015B/2285